I Closed My Eyes

M.Q. JACKSON

TRAFFORD

CANADA • UK • IRELAND • USA • SPAIN

PRINTED IN VICTORIA, CANADA

National Library of Canada Cataloguing in Publication Data

A cataloguing record for this book that includes the U.S. Library of Congress Classification number, the Library of Congress Call number and the Dewey Decimal cataloguing code is available from the National Library of Canada. The complete cataloguing record can be obtained from the National Library's online database at: www.nlc-bnc.ca/amicus/index-e.html

ISBN 1-4120-3071-4

TRAFFORD

THIS BOOK WAS PUBLISHED ON-DEMAND IN COOPERATION WITH TRAFFORD PUBLISHING. ON-DEMAND PUBLISHING IS A UNIQUE PROCESS AND SERVICE OF MAKING A BOOK AVAILABLE FOR RETAIL SALE TO THE PUBLIC TAKING ADVANTAGE OF ON-DEMAND MANUFACTURING AND INTERNET MARKETING. ON-DEMAND PUBLISHING INCLUDES PROMOTIONS, RETAIL SALES, MANUFACTURING, ORDER FULFILMENT, ACCOUNTING AND COLLECTING ROYALTIES ON BEHALF OF THE AUTHOR.

Suite 6E, 2333 Government St., Victoria, B.C. V8T 4P4, CANADA
Phone 250-383-6864 • Toll-free 1-888-232-4444 (Canada & US)
Fax 250-383-6804 • E-mail sales@trafford.com
Web site: www.trafford.com
TRAFFORD PUBLISHING IS A DIVISION OF TRAFFORD HOLDINGS LTD.
Trafford Catalogue #04-0898   www.trafford.com/robots/04-0898.html

10   9   8   7   6   5   4   3   2

Table of Contents

Acknowledgements

Comments from my family and friends are the strongest form of encouragement. I wish to express my sincerest appreciation to Karen Brown and Joann Wiley for taking time out of their busy schedules to listen to my poetry. I would also like to thank Orville Clarke, Frank Jama, Kenshaw Stephens, Tanisha Davis, Jaymie Brinkmeier, Shimira Jackson, Paul Gearson, Kim Liferidge, Donna Coakley, Micah Webb, William Coakley, Terry Austin and Marsharee Austin, Kizzy Duncan, Eugene Alexander, Alexis Brown, Johnny Holiday, Andrea Petrovani, Tylesha Allen, Julie Thompson, Terrence Cherry, Ronald and Carla Craig, Hannah Samae Dorsey, Keith Washington, Deidra Calloway, Brenda Kitrell all in which are selfless friends who gave support during this venture in arranging my collage of poems.

I am grateful for my family's faithful support. Mr. And Mrs. Alonza Gordon, Leonard Jackson, Kenneth Jackson, and Gerald Jackson thank you kindly.

Last but not least, I would like to thank a special someone for introducing me to love and pain, which put me on the emotional roller coaster ride leading me to this final destination of redemption.

Dedication

I sincerely would like to take the time out to specially thank Clifton Knight, Terrence Cherry, Tony Ross, and Jack Yelder. You guy's were there for me in ways un-imaginable. During the tough times after my separation I had a place to live. Terrence you gave up your apartment and paid the bills so that I could live comfortable. "Thanks"

Cliff AKA "Big Sak" Thanks for letting me crash on your sofa and the many talks we've shared. Tony, What can I say thanks for the sofa and the many nights of hanging to take my mind off my messy situation. Jack Marvin Yelder, I thank you for trusting me and supporting me through it all. "thanks for the apartment"

I can't forget those Galley boy's at NAS JAX. HAPPY, BO, CLEM, K.J, RUTH, CURRY. The 2-5 click.

Rodney Thomas who showed me when life gives you lemons, make Lemonade.

Karen Brown, Joanne Wiley and Brenda Kitrell. Thanks from the bottom of my heart. For giving me that extra boost of confidence. "I did it".

Aunt Alice, mommy, Rosetta, Juanita Edwards, Gerald and Linda Jackson thanks for keeping me in your prayers.

Some how with the love from all of you made this book possible thank you and I love you all.

Inspiration

Shimira you have inspired me to write this book of poems. Our massive break-up really tore me up; in essence it taught me how to connect with what my feelings really were. Once I found out that love was more than words uttered, and not forever promised. I then was able to share with the world spoken word from the heart. Thank you for loving me when you did and thank you for the pain you imposed upon me. I now am a better person who understands more about the life that I was dealt. I forgive you and I will always love you in that special way.

I Write

By: Marcus Q. Jackson

I write because I like the feeling of being free
An intellectual form of expression,
Expressing the real true meaning of this image you see of me.
See in poem I escape prisons and climb skyscrapers
I pour secrets of my heart out rhythmically onto paper.
Saying words I could never build the courage to say
Like I think of you baby every waking day.
Or the fact that love left me when I begged of her to stay.

I write on most sleepless nights
When experiencing the feeling
Feelings of when things are just not right.
So I fight with reality and I write
To make things right
To end all my sleepless nights
I write to give pain shape
And love substance when her heart breaks
When left all alone with no one to turn to
Feeling sad and blue
I write for you.

How can I tell you what I really feel?
I write
Ensuring every word is precise and every gesture is clear
When I speak somehow the real words linger behind

But when I write it's easy to say I find
You interesting and you're always on my mind.

Shy choosing the role of friend
When the real words I love you and I want you
Are trapped in bondage within
Until that sleepless night
When I write.
Destroying my nemesis
Shedding tears
Through ink I make pain disappear
And unconditional love appear
Surreal.

I write to mirror myself
The footnotes of my eulogy at my awaited death
No interest in wealth
I write for you and the freedom of myself.

Tomorrow

By: Marcus Q. Jackson

I awake today
Realizing today was really yesterday
A replay,
Of the redundancy I display as yesterday
A sitcom of sorrow
With hope of tomorrow
Voided heart soulfully hollow
Will tomorrow ever come an relieve me
From the filth of yesterdays stale air and soiled thoughts
And break bondage of what time caught
Yet I yield to the room of stagnation and sorrow
All alone with visions of tomorrow

I stand at my window and I see
I see families holding hands walking through the park,
Birds singing flying by
Mothers breast feeding their newborns
And I ask why?
I see construction of new homes, Dads outside barbecuing
Moms in the kitchen making sides
Kids out back running around
Then comes the sound
The sound of reality beating the tune of misery
Selfish misery who must always have company

Should I be fortunate because misery chose me
I turn to speak sliding to the floor with my face in hand
I asked misery why, because I really didn't understand.
Why can't I go into tomorrow like others
And rid my mind of all my troubles
Yet misery adds to my depression more troubles.

Father, are you coming?
I hear a whisper through the walls
My son called to me from tomorrow
I yelled as I stood up; yes son
But he couldn't hear my call
I fell to a skirmish crawl
Leaning against the wall,
Carving in another day,
Another day that's today but really yesterday
Dad? I hear him again
This time I couldn't answer
Misery muzzled my mouth and whispered into my mind
I'm your only friend
Get use to today because tomorrow will never come again.
You've called to your God
And you see he never came
Leaving you helpless and bonded in these chains

Ha ha ha I hear laughter outside my window
A couple watching home videos of yesterday
Comparing to their life of today
A new day, tomorrow they made it

While I continue to sit
They held each other close rendering a passionate kiss so soft
The man grabbed the remote and turned yesterday off.
I think to myself, wow, a vivid thought in mind
I picked up my remote to find that it only worked in play and
rewind.
I threw it against the wall for surely now I'm forever stuck in time
Now all hope is gone no longer I fight with sorrow
I await death, my only way to get to tomorrow.

Fallen Petals

By: Marcus Q. Jackson

Unique it was, a black rose
Living amongst the flamboyant array
Of orchids in the field of dreams
Showing vivid colors
Shielding the beauty of this unique rose
It seemed.

Leaving her heart broken, I suppose
Her true beauty she was not allowed to show
Slowly dying from the weeds not allowing her to grow
Cautious as I approached this sadden rose
Slowly dying amongst the unpleasantness of those
Who camouflaged her essence and sheer beauty
For no one else to see
But, for that one night
I saw an un-imaginable beauty

Clipping the weeds from the rose
Her blooms started to blossom and her stem started to grow
Surprising, to the rose
It had thorns, petals and a color to which it didn't even know.
She was smiling and swaying in the spark
Of the moon light
For once everything was all right

And no one seemed to care
Making wishes upon the stars through out the earth's atmosphere

Holding the red rose close
I embraced her with love
Not love of passion
But the love of letting her know
The feeling of being special
If fate had it to be I whispered
It's your love that I will treasure

Silence filled the air
With anticipated hope
The petals of the red rose leaned into my chest and silently spoke
Before we part from this night
I want you to know that you will always have a place in my heart
It's unfortunate that we are trapped between two worlds
And to my world I'm not willing to part
For my love is to the array
And I will sooner die, than to leave it astray
I wept quietly and whispered
Remember the black petals for they are not far away.

FREEDOM

By: Marcus Jackson
Dedication to Tanisha Davis

Freedom, I danced in my black dress for Freedom.
The stars burned bright on this crystal night of Freedom.
I finally saw him.
A virtuous man, a precious gem,
I need him.
A wish I never thought would come,
Could he be the one?

His smile lit up the dance floor.
His laughter forever poured.
This man I wanted more,
His actions I so adored.
He's my freedom.

Behind these invisible bars
He's the twinkle that lights my stars
He's that love that makes life so hard!
But IS he the love worth fighting for?
Could he be my Freedom behind these closed doors?

I try to ignore,
The letters, the calls, the silence on the floor
I sometimes imagine what freedom means to him.
Am I his moon and stars and virtuous gem?

Or is he an abstract photo that I've given life?
Or this mere dream of becoming someone's wife:
Or am I the heart waiting to be stabbed by his knife?

I'm in jail never did I think twice.
He is my life,
And I am willing to be his wife.
I will roll the dice.
He's worth the sacrifice

Lucky 7, the fate of my life
Parole! It's time to go.
Should I stay or should I go?
FREEDOM!
Please, I beg of you, to let me know!

Awaiting My Sunshine

By: Marcus Q. Jackson

Dark as a midnight Forrest my dearest
The clearest sound holds no voice
So hear this
Weeping cry a pitch so high
Awaiting the sun until I die
A lonely death of a sadden heart
Torn from separation so far apart
A brisk wind blows
With no sound of yours
Leaving a pain I couldn't ignore
Shine on me so bright tonight
Let me know that all is right
Give me that bright golden glow
To dry my river and control it's flow
Rivers running wild with no damn in view
Hear me cry as I cry for you.

Me

By: Marcus Q. Jackson

In thought
I think of being an encyclopedia
Having all the answers
A rare an precious jewel
On display
A super hero saving the day
A map to show you the way
The tear-jerking scene that stole the show
That special place that you love to go
The suave dancer serenading the dance floor
A bottomless bottle of your favorite wine
That will forever pour

I want to be that dream that makes you smile in your sleep
The reality to your anticipated fantasy
The good news that made you forever happy
I want to be your everlasting desire
But I can only be me

Someone who will love you for eternity
Invisible to infidelity
A sanctuary for your security
Infinite Passion religiously
That star that shines vividly
This is the reality

Of all I perceive to be
When you chose me
These things I promised to be
Your universe
The Heavens and the earth
Your planet of truth and infinity

Complain

By: Marcus Q. Jackson

I started complaining today
Un-happy with life
Taking every breath for granted
I felt a bit disenchanted
Un-satisfied but I didn't understand it
I'm breathing I'm seeing I'm walking I'm talking
I'm living
But why am I complaining about this life that I'm given

Tomorrow is not promised
Yet I still complain
For I alone endure pain
Until I felt the rain
Showering in others pain

My cousin passed away sometime ago she was only sixteen
My aunt was hysterical
The next week she lost her husband and it wasn't a dream
Now she's alone fighting to live life
And I complain never thinking twice

My friend Dominique and his sister Nichole were murdered
Years apart
Leaving their kids and parents
Motherless, fatherless, childless with a broken heart

My friend lost his job today not knowing where his next meal would
be coming from
Contemplated suicide fear of becoming a bum
Down on himself, thinking about his wife and son

My cousin was convicted today for a murder he didn't commit
Now living aimlessly behind bars on a twenty year sentence

So many stories and so many are sad
Now I know why I complained
Because today at work
My boss made me mad
My son didn't call me dad
And my wife didn't ask me what kind of day I had
So, I complain and I still ask why
A tear fell from the sky
I sadden God and made him cry
Why?

The Stage

By: Marcus Q. Jackson

Soft settled rainbow flowers
Backdrops the window
As she stood quietly gazing out at the stage
Performers stood by
Tears without eyes to cry
Mechanical birds soared the sky
With the intent to honorably die

The Towers came fallen down
Dancers danced the rhythm of chaotic sound
Mournful was the town
The cast lied still the stage
Tri-colored garment burned celebrating the rage

Gunfire in celebration
Gunfire for devastation
Guns fired 21 salutes in commemoration

The narrator speaks
For every tear that silently dropped
The curtains closed to set up new props

Wet waters and dusty trails
Evil in the air let God prevail
Fire burning black clouds of smoke

Black gold says the joke
Stingers flying by piercing the skin
A feel of homelessness
Wondering if they will ever see home again
Cannons blaring toward foreign land
Young men and women cry
Because they didn't understand

Safe is the narrator tonight
Watching outside the stage
Watching the performers blindly fight
Pregnant birds of evil took flight
Giving birth in the sky
Falling to the stage killing everyone standing by

New scene new prop
New mission on communist rock
Bound in chains spiritual believers
Praying non-stop

Dark wilting flowers
Backdrops the window
As she stood grieving
Towards the stage
ENDURING FREEDOM!

Black Jesus

By: Marcus Q. Jackson

Would it matter if Jesus were black
Judging from the ancient artifacts
Hieroglyphics on walls
Would it matter that Jesus were black
Does it change the fact?
Of this condition we're in
Would it matter if Jesus were white?
Would you not have him as your closet friend?
I say again
Would it really matter if Jesus were black?
Would it stop?
The luding, polluting, stabbings and shootings
The trife the stealing
Child molestation and drug dealing
Plane hi-jacking, terrorist attacking
Parents slacking
Child abduction, clinic disruption
A world of mass corruption
Sars, Aids
Cancerous cells, kids in graves?
Now would it matter if Jesus were black?
Did he stop ancient facts
Of whites enslaving blacks?
Or did he turn the flood from Nubia
Preserving ancient artifacts?

Proving that he the Messiah is really black
But does it matter that Jesus is black
I say No!
It's time to wake and acknowledge the faith
The faith that eliminate self and expounded hate
The faith that will show you the way
Of survival to another thankful day
God makes no mistakes.
Would it matter if Jesus were black?
Or an Anglo-sax
Does it erase the fact?
That he died for you and me
And we're blinded by the colors so that we can't see
The true coming of Christ
Was to save our life
Yet we worry about color
And not the sacrifice
Would it matter that Jesus were black, white, Hispanic, Asian or Jew.
It shouldn't because Jesus is you.

Hennessy

By: Marcus Q. Jackson

Your perfectly defined body decants the smoothness of your flow
Exposing the essence of sheer beauty
Manifesting the brightness of your glow
Allow me to apologize but I must introduce myself
I see strange men conversing
By chance would there be any conversation left
Would you mind if I hold you close
And introduce you to my friends and propose a toast.

To us Henny and Jack
Crystal tumblers and fine cognac
Smoked fill rooms rhythmic poetic heat
Reaching mike Phillips through a quantum jazz beat

Consuming your flavor,
No lie baby it's a flavor to savor
The touch of your smoothness is major
It's kismet that we met
Your warm kisses makes me sweat
Leaving my insides wet.

Would you like to dance, come on girl let's tour
The dance floor,
But before we go baby give me some more.
Of that treasure most men die for

It's not normal someone as fancy as you sitting at my table
I guess tonight I should be on my best behavior.
But damn you look so good
I mean, you are the best looking woman I've ever seen
You kind of look like that model in essence magazine.

Your voice are like chimes ringing the sweet sounds of jingles
Twirling your smooth essence with my fingers
As long as you are by my side Henny I could never go wrong
I mean you relax my soul and turn my weaknesses strong.

I wish for this night to never end, but I'm fresh out of cigarettes and
Ben Franklins.
The conversation was nice but it's business as usual right .
Well hopefully I will see you again next weekend
I leave, but your spirits are lost within me
The way you warm my heart makes it easy
For me to say that I love you Hennessy.

Drowning

By: Marcus Q Jackson

As the water become deeper
I slowly watch myself drowning
The wall seemed so far away
As I held my breath
Trying to make it through another day

I'm killing myself

Why do I jump in the deep and cannot swim
Why do I continue and try
Every day again and again
Where are the lifeguards?
Where is the floatation device?
Where is the plug to drain the pool?
I'm drowning
Helplessly consumed loosing my life
The depths has the drunken fool

Blurred vision
Restless body
Help me please somebody
The currents are too strong
I'm drifting out to sea
Miserably tired floating aimlessly

How could shallow water
Become so rough
One shot
Turned to overflowing rivers and streams
Panic is my screams
Help!! Help me please

Lord, give me the strength to swim free
Plant my feet on solid ground
To stand against the sin
Out from the contaminated water
I will never swim again

Then there's tomorrow
Thinking, of how it feels to swim
Slowly floating
In search for Atlantis
Free of worries and cares
I can't stop,
I want to reach Atlantis
All I desire rest there

The more I swim the closer I come
The deeper I go the more I forget
How, do I return to where I'm from
I'm a slave to the ocean
Took from the pool
Send a boat for the drowning fool

Precious Wind

By: Marcus Q. Jackson

Let not the source of life be consumed
I ask for one more chance
To baste in the wind
The invisible life source
Fed by God through his umbilical cord
Of no end
I take hold of the wind

Behind The Blinds

By: Marcus Q. Jackson

I can feel the energy in the room
A gravitational pull
Keeping me grounded, blinded from reality
I hear peace and feel sound.
I listen with feeling
Isolating the mind, thoughts of the heart
I've defined love.

I feel sound as it penetrates my soul
Steady rain drops flow
Sweet whistles as the wind passes
Taxiing the sound of nature below.
The surface of flesh
Through the tunnels of life
In search of truth
The unseen light
For I'm feeing sound without view
I'm feeling you.

To the surprise of the opening of the blinds
Sound went away
Runny faucet, rotating fan, therapeutic chimes
Visually suspended sound.

I Just Want To Talk

By: Marcus Q. Jackson

I'm at a loss for words
I would like to say something
I want to explain what I feel

I can't speak
These feelings are unique
I want to write about what happened this week

Where is everyone
Does anyone care to know how I feel
My feelings are surreal
God here's the deal

I'm lonely, I'm sad
I smile but I'm confused and mad
I want to understand these feelings that I feel
Are they forever
Or am I dreaming, and the feelings aren't for real

Will you ever wake me from this nightmare
Of fatal thoughts of ending it all
Slowly by the consumption of alcohol

I give up
I don't care anymore
I guess when it rains it really does pour

So many advance and move on
So many have a victorious song
So many of my rights have gone wrong
So many days now I have walked alone

I just want to talk

And tell you that yesterday
I thought about dying
I couldn't take it anymore
Trying to live in this world
So I stopped trying
To no avail
I was found lying

In the same spot I contemplated suicide
In my bed alive
It was just a thought
I really don't want to die
But how much longer shall I try
For happiness in my life

Do you know I really don't like the way my life has turned out
It's so confusing I don't even know what it's all about

That's the shit that makes me want to shout
Lord what is it really about

Am I suppose to preach and teach
Well who is it that I'm suppose to reach
Why must I help everyone with their life
When mine is so bleak
Someone please talk with me

I just want to talk

Maybe your words can set me free
From this confined misery
That has held me to be
Strange fruit hanging from a Mississippi tree

Judge ye not
But I'm judged a lot
Somehow I don't fit into the slot
In societies parking lot
I've given this filthy world all that I've got

The Love the honor and commitment
To my fellow man
To be spit on
Now this is the part I don't understand
Now it's time to take a stand
And break the band
And pull back my hand

With my love I curse you
Never again shall you use me
And abuse me
You have confused me
The rapture is coming you will soon see
I have been more to you than I have been to myself
With my love I curse you to death
I just need someone to talk to
And ask why
Why? When so hard I try
So many tears I cry
Watching the days of sorrow roll on by

When I do for them
How come they don't do for me
Life's not fair
And it's plain to see
Maybe this is how you have written it to be

Enough conversation
Thanks for the talk
My destiny I shall walk
And collect my thoughts
Thanks for letting me talk

Imagine How God Feels

By: Marcus Q. Jackson

Was I not there when you called to me
Was I not there when you needed me
Was I not there when you were trapped and I set you free
So many voices call my name
So many tears fell like rain
So much heartache when feeling your pain
Enough with the abuse
It's driving me insane
Stop calling my name
With my love brings upon a curse
You should have not taken my love in vain

The End Of The Beginning

By: Marcus Q Jackson

Trumpet blows, silence lurk
Unimaginable sight, massive hurt
Pain unknown, such misery shown
Reaping souls, the here and the gone
Tears fall upon un-faithful souls
the bleeding earth holds,
The then and the now.
Beast awaits its loyal prey
the rapture it's announced
Ye who goes and ye who stays
pleading on Christ's deaf ears
Vanishes, his light
lost and alone in darkness
comes the anti-Christ.

I Knock

By: Marcus Q. Jackson

I walked away from heavens' hand
To rejoin man
With the impression that God
Our God just didn't understand

The pain and pressure that life was dealing
And how the outside was looking more and more appealing
Having thoughts of being ignored every night I went kneeling.

Into prayer where I'd shed lots of lonely tears
No instant answer from the Divine
I felt my prayers were falling upon deaf ears
So it appeared, nothing seemed clear

I ask why God? I never missed a service in church
I even witnessed on the street corner
Giving my testimony but somehow that didn't work

I can't take it no longer my desires are getting stronger
On bended knees Lord I'm calling upon ya
If you really exist then stop me from thinking this way
No sign from the Divine, so I walked away
Into the wilderness becoming demonic prey
A worse state of being than I was in yesterday.

So I prayed above my grave
Murdered by the Gods of sin my life enslaved
Metal bracelets shackled feet
Horrific visions no retreat
Lonely nights darkened rooms sounds of the streets
Boom!! Another life consumed

No quiet corners no place to think
Propositioned by the sin God offering a drink
He said that it would help me think
So I drank.

Blurred vision no worries no cares
No concern of yesterday, today, tomorrow,
Non existent no longer were they there

I live for now alone on this spiritual quest
Trying to find a home for my soul to rest
At the foot steps of my Father's house
Yelled out, go from here!
For you have not completed thy test

You shall withstand all that you've taken for granted and more.
You will become doubtless of the things you've doubted before
You will cry in disgrace and sorrow as you stand before each exit door

The cards of sin you've dealt shall return ten times ten
You will reap every shortcoming again and again.

When you walked away from me it was like a dog returning to his
own vomit
or a cleansed pig waddling upon his stomach

For if you had been of me
no doubt that you would have continued with me
I fell to my knees, Lord please! Why has thou forsaken me?

Answered
Nor have I left or forsaken thee
When you find the true meaning of life then right here shall I be

The burning words seeped within my soul through my chest
Piercing my heart
A true sign from the Divine to devour my flesh
From a deep sleep I arose in shock
I read Romans chapter 8 and silently I knocked.

I Choose You

By: Marcus Q Jackson

Sleepless nights with you in mind
My moon my stars
My sun that shines
Every waking day I try and find
The words to explain how I feel
To let you know you are always on my mind
I choose you because you are the one
And I confirm that these feelings are for real

I choose you

Because you are a queen in my eyes
Caramel cutie
Can't you see how hard I try
Baby I tell no lie
If I had wings I would fly
Across the sky
In search for you until the day I die
I choose you because I need you
To complete myself
I will wait beyond death
I absorb your soul
Within my lost heart
Seeking cleanliness

To sanitize the mystery
That may be keeping us apart

I choose you

Because you are pure
Natural, loving, caring, sharing, daring
Angel wings you're wearing
Queen of the night
Out of sight
I choose you
Because it feels so right
Take my hand and walk with me
Share my soul
My soul mate till eternity
Infinity
Further than your eyes could see

I choose you
Because you are right for me
Look through my eyes to my soul
Because it holds the true story

I choose you
Soon I hope one day you will choose me too

Red Velvet Cake

By: Marcus Q Jackson

Thirst quenching moisture
Divided, revealing the essence of calmness within
Basting in sugary sweet frosting
Anticipation, I can't wait to dig in.

The layers of sweetness invited my touch
The texture was elegant soft and plush
An uncontrollable yearning of situational lust

I'm starved for the sweetness
It's been awhile since having a slice of cake
Freshly baked
I closed my eyes! Umm I could taste
The aroma that lingers throughout the place

Lying a slice upon my plate
Dripping frosting aside my lips
Seductively I ate

The sugary sweet taste satisfying my appetite
So satisfying I yearned for one more bite
Warming my internal core this long awaited night
The flavor was just right

As I slid my fork between the creamy white icing
Into the red velvety core
Melting inside I begged for more
Of the essence I so desperately adored
Fallen to the floor
Physically erect the quintessential taste
I couldn't ignore
Rolling in joy consuming more

Externally I erupt
Lying lifeless as the sugary sweet frosting massively began to pour
All over the kitchen floor
I put the cake away in a safe place for when I hunger
I could come back for more.

Funny Little Valentine

By: Marcus Q. Jackson

Chocolate cream pie
Sweet as the vanilla sky
Marshmallow clouds passing by
Raindrops lemony sweet
Cherry teardrops
Baste my feet
Candy shelled heart
Filled with flowing love
The essential part
For eternal love
Sweet chocolate lips
Glazed in strawberry gloss
Peppermint smile
A moment not to be lost
My funny little valentine
Harmonic melodies plays Cupids wind chime
Floating on a velvet line
Everlasting joy
Everlasting mine
For everlasting time
Everlasting memories
My funny little Valentine
Raspberry Ocean
Coconut streams
Red roses and violets

Manifested sight
In this blind mans dream
Dipped in sweet caramel
Covered in hazel nuts
Sweet tasting valentine
Explosive was the nut
My funny little Valentine
I'm grateful that you are mine

Thug Girl

By: Marcus Q. Jackson

Pulling hard on that Newport
Blowing smoke out into the atmosphere
She's different
Her appearance is a bit surreal
Who is this lady and what's the deal
Could such a bizarre creature make me feel
Drawing me close with her amazing sex appeal
For real what is the deal?

She smiled staring deep into my eyes
No disguise
Then I realized, this girl was not of lies
Looking down, amazed of her soft and luscious thighs

So I made a choice
I wanted to hear this creature's voice
To a coins toss
Heads or tails
Heads I win tails I fail
I freshened my game
I can't step to her stale

Micro-braids, Jordan sneaks, Denim skirt
I must say this girl was very unique
And required some work

She stood tough thumping ashes to the ground
She was in a world of her on
As if no one was around
She was hella fine crip walking around
Throwing deuces to the sound
Of Snoop D. O double G
And the dog pound

I wanted to know of this un-known creature
In my world
I had to ask. What are you?
She replied by saying I'm a thug girl

I was unsure what to say next
But she read me like a book
As if she had written the text

She knew my desire
Extinguishing my fire
Offered me her body for hire
Roll playing
I called her my servant
And she called me sire

I pleased her
Bathing her body in wine
For that moment
This servant was finally and completely mines
Enjoying her everlasting essence from behind

The taste of her kiss was sweet
Newport smoke and cognac
Rubbing fingers down her angelic back
I was on that
She moaned into my ear moaning my name
Ooh Jack

Pleasure in the atmosphere
As she rocked my world
It wasn't a dream
I was lost in the world of a Thug girl

Genitalia

By: Marcus Q. Jackson

Manifested power defines this great magnitude
Of passion and pain, magnetic forces
To allude the brains
Mental depressions, deep transgressions, hidden obsessions
Honesty, love, and faithfulness
Surely I questioned.

When faced with the enemy
Who appears so friendly?
Rendered smiles vividly
Genitalia can always see
The desires of others heart
Enticing,
Sometimes so enticing
it starts and breaks relationships apart.

It's the two- headed coin of good and bad
The creator of feelings, those happy and sad
Such desire! Transforming priest to liars
Had Sampson fall for Delilah
Careful, sometimes it burns like fire.

Penis rise standing strong to part the vaginal sea
Her pink cage bird sings
From the stinging of his bee

Blood flow pumping camel back humping
Weak in the knees slumping
A retreat of dismay
With the thought of knowing you've left something.
Which was the wrong thing?
Un-expected part of your life long dream
Then comes the screams from your previous scene
Reality, mommy and daddy at age sixteen

Or maybe husband and wife
Cut by the adulterers' knife.
Long awaited passage through the hidden tunnel
Finally the true essence within
It's wonderful
Entering her tunnel again and again

Walls of moisture strategically place
Devouring her smoothness at a slow snails pace
Clinched hands, furrowed face
Oh God echoes throughout the place
A moment stuck in time never to be erased.

Genitalia
Is greatly desired by every kind
Powers to change the average mind
Impulses that makes father question time.

Genitalia
It's a wolf in sheep's clothing
And sometimes the opposite
So eagerly anticipated
Some forgot to check the letter and the mailbox
Before making their deposit.

Sorry you can't return to sender
When you found that you and Gina are of the same gender.
Or the fact that he left an unwanted guests
Trapped within ya.

It's the good the bad
The happy the sad
The cheerful the mad
It's the mom and the dad
The beginning of this end
It's the enemy as well as a great friend.

Addicted

By: Marcus Q. Jackson

Sh Sh Sh
Stop! Go away leave me alone
No! No! Don't do this to me
Please stop calling my name
You're driving me in sane!
Think man Think
Try and maintain
It's the Demon playing with your brain
Block it out, block it out
God help me! Please take away the pain

Hm hm hm crying,
Tears dropped to the floor
Shaking nervously aside the bed
Rationalizing with the thoughts
Dancing through my head

I have no control over my mind
I feel as though I'm dying
I need it, I need a fix
All I need is one hit
Shit!

Hm hm hm crying

Be strong
Don't think about it
Be strong
Breaking shit throwing shit

I can't be strong
The shit's calling me
It will not leave me the fuck alone
Stop calling my name, stop calling my name
Please stop calling my name
Sliding across the floor to the closet –door
Reaching for the 38 to blow out my brain

I'm going crazy, enough of the anger
I pulled back the trigger
Click!! Empty was the chamber
You can't get rid of me
Voices the voices
Who are you? Where are you?
You are you. Here are you.
There's no stranger

Get up, get up and go and make that money
You deserve some of that sweet tasting honey
Go out there and turn a few tricks
Smoke a few bricks
No more pain and no more feeling sick
So what if you have to suck a few dicks
Isn't it worth it?

Yeah you're right
After all it's only for one night
And I can feel high as a kite.

Dark streets; abandon buildings
A dollar I got to make
Zombies migrating we all looking for the take
Jones'n , my heart ache
My body nervously shakes
As I sexually satisfied eight

Popping spit for one more hit
Fantasying about it
My last hit
I died high as the kite
Living the life of an addict.

Lieutenant

By: Marcus Q. Jackson
Dedicated to Andrea & Johnny

If dreams came true,
My life, I would have you in it
A most high Diva
But I'm forced to call you lieutenant.
Swaying the hallways with that New York strut
Defining every inch of those Khakis
Jeopardizing that soft chiseled butt
I'll give anything just for one touch
A soft touch that I long so much
They ask me who that is
I answer, the New York chick from Trinidad
Who drives me mad?
Not knowing rather to say hello Ma'am
Or yell out, L T baby girl you are bad.
With your sensual smile complimented by your earthly complexion
It's enough to give any man an erection
I'm sorry belaying my last as I stand down at attention.
Let me speak my mind for this one night
Tell you how I would wine and dine
And make you feel alright.
Sincerity, when we ask you to stay
I Jack the Ripper and Doc Holliday.
LT don't forget the names
Now that you are leaving we're retired from this game

Because when you look too the left and you look to your right
Hell it's all the same

Hypocrite

By: Marcus Q. Jackson

I'm tired of you people judging me
You don't even know me
Pushing your thoughts and views
Upon me trying to control me

When did it become a concern about what I do?
Check yourself! You're phony
And I can't stand you

Self-righteous hypocrite
Your life is a contradict
Get out my face you make me sick
To my stomach
You make me wonna vomit
Pretending to be innocent
Your life's a joke
Why would I want it?

You're no better than I am
For once stand up and be a man or woman
Got damn

Must we always play this game?
I'm better than you are
I look better than you do

Girl he can't do nothing for me
You're right cause I wouldn't do shit for you
Swank wonna be
You lost touch with reality
Living for society
Causing me grief

Saturday night humping
Sunday bible thumping
Drunk at the bar on Monday trying to tell me something

I mean who are you?
Trying to deface me
Your perception of life is crazy
Your kind, never cease to amaze me

To feel big you try and make others feel small
Coward, cringing inside behind a callous wall
Full time fraud
Part time praising the lord
You have been erased I pulled the cord

On your kind
Never will you reach my mind
I don't care if you hate the fact that
I'm short and black
And my bank rolls not stack
You're blind and vain
Your kind can't see beyond that.

Careful when you're judging me
You might end up ten times worse than you perceive me to be.
Living a Coward's life feeding on hypocrisy

Spiritual In This Material World

By: Marcus Q. Jackson

Ideologies, ideas, eye tears
I fear what's near
Coming here

Random death from thyself
Diminishing wealth
Leaving nothing left.

Chasing the dream
Drifting down stream
Floating away I scream

Dissatisfaction, translation dissatisfied
Disappointed my fantasies died
I find that true love lingers inside
Once hidden behind shallow walls of pride
Sheltered from the outside

Not allowed to move on and overlook the appearance
Of the exterior
Protecting a reputation
A reputation that's inferior

To change, and societal beliefs
A belief that kept me beneath
Life and its material grief

Ladies seeking them six foot tall
Chiseled chest and all
Fellas are seeking their Halle Berry
And Drag's, their RuPaul.

Tommy, Fubu, Sean John
And Guess.
Admit it's not the fit
It's the shit
That gives you clear passage through societies test

Bentleys, Roll's, Escalades, Navagades
All produces slaves
Corrupted from the cradle to the grave
Snoop Dogg, D.R.E, Tupac and B.I.G
All were slaves
Now two are set free

Escaping the material wealth
Through death
Life is for living now free yourself.

Life Let Me Live

By: Marcus Q. Jackson

With my eyes wide open I walked to my death
Willing and able
Church bells ringing
Children singing
The unveiling clothe
My nerves were tingling
Uncertain to what life was bringing

His touch of kindness made me complete
I was given things
Classic and unique
I was special! Placed upon a pedestal
Crowned and bowed upon
Announced throughout the world
That I was his queen
The chosen one

Life's servants submissive to my beck and call
Giving me anything I desired
It was wonderful on the other side
It was wonderful, until the fall
In search of knowing how to crawl

Life was loosing himself
Begging me to stop his pain

I had not the answer
I wanted no longer the ring
Life gave me a shape
I had no shape of my own
Life was always there
Never leaving me to do on my own
Life begged me to stay
My soul begged to be gone

I love you life
You are so kind to me
That's why I ask of you
To let me go free
So I can find me
I must go it's something I must do
Life please let me live
And give back the life I've given you.

Lifeless I Lay

By: Marcus Q. Jackson

Lying lifeless
My legs levitate
My worth is dirt, scared and confused
Without a choice to choose

My heart aches
Eyes like puddles fill with liquid pain
Red paint covered the white canvas
Revealing my pain

Clinched hands furrowed face
Punctured wounds
The blood I can taste
The sounds of sorrow filtered throughout the place

Lying lifeless
I ask God. Why?
Staring at my baby dolls
And they began to cry
Wishing for God to come down from the sky
Tears, Tears, Tears
Lord please tell me why

Ice cream, my favorite Sponge Bob Ice cream
I dreamed
Licking it up and down all over dancing around
Wiping away the sticky cream

Running from my uncle I scream
No! With my mouth full of ice cream
To wake and realize it's not a dream
I'm still here in this painful scene

Mommy
Mommy where are you?
I need you, Mommy please
No! No! No!
Stop it Please! Get off of me
Screaming yelling out loud
No sound to expound
I was screaming internally

I'm so weak Lord. Lay my soul to rest
I felt this rough surface
Rub across my smooth leveled chest
When I heard the voice speak
You've almost past the test

Hush now don't you say a word to anyone
Uncle was only having a little fun
Now go and clean yourself up
And remember don't say a thing

And uncle will bring you back
Your favorite Sponge Bob ice cream

I smiled filling my tummy with all different color candies
One after another
Writing a letter to my mother and her brother
I lay lifeless in peace from all my troubles
Then I saw the light.
I heard my Mothers voice crying out
Thank you Jesus my baby girl is going to be all right.

Friend

By: Marcus Q Jackson
Dedication from Jaymie to Sharon

I can honestly say I've met a friend today
Someone I could talk too
When I am feeling low
Someone who isn't afraid to tell me no
This one person I call friend
I'm sad to see go

Many late night talks
Analyzing the drama
Some brought
So many wonderful memories
So much, that time has caught

You are a true friend
It's funny but I remember how it all began
I told you a secret
And I never heard that secret again
You make it so easy
To call you friend

Your heart is like a jewel to me
I promise to cherish our friendship
For eternity, infinity
Some can't begin to see

By having you around
Made my life easy

I think of the future
Never forgetting the past
Our friendship was built on trust
And with trust
It will forever last

You're kind, you're humble, you're loving, you're caring
I will truly miss you Sharon
Things will never be the same
Without hearing your name
Ya'll give it up
To my friend Sharon
AKA Soul train

William Blake

By: Marcus Q. Jackson

I obtain visions of beautiful Angels
And ghostly Monks
I converse with the Angel Gabriel
And the Virgin Mary
Adhering to their wants

The year of our Lord 1757
Begat this London mystic
A militant pro-founding individualist
Detesting institutionalized religion
For I am God sent

Imagine, imagination, internal
The human imagination
Is the sole means of expressing the Eternal

We the divine image
The possessors of human virtues
Mercy, pity, peace and love
Portrait of marriage between heaven and hell
Hanging above

Yet we are a fallen people
Not from God but ourselves

The path to liberation lies inside each of us
And no one else

We need not wait for one greater man
For our salvation is a personal one
Ironically prevented by the
Limitations we place on ourselves.
And then some

I'm a poor man striving
English poet, painter, and engraver
Mystical mind of our profound savior
For I dictate my future
Through my own behavior

Little lamb who made thee
Does thou know who made thee
Tyger! Tyger! Burning bright
In the forest of the night
In what distant deeps or skies
Burnt the fire of thine eyes
The year of our lord 1827
Was the demise

A mystic, suffering great poverty
Who wants the world to see
The little lamb who made thee.

Imnowhere

By: Marcus Q. Jackson

I didn't have time
I did not see the end
People told me
But the sound was un-certain
Behind the draped curtain
Is this really the end?
Or is it the time to begin again?
Can I right my wrong of sin?

Lost in space
Such an unfamiliar place
Staring me in the face
It's nowhere
I'm lost in nowhere
With tribulations to share

I can see yesterday
As if it was moments away
What might have happen, to bring me this way?
Lifeless I lay
And the preacher began to pray.
I'm nowhere
Or am I now here.

Fly Angel

By: Marcus Q. Jackson
Dedication to Kayren Gooden

Confined in the mind of confusion
Turning to the divine for the solution
Of this confusion,

I close my eyes in the hope of a new tomorrow
Happiness of my own not a happiness I have to borrow.

I'm confused, but why, I'm lost but I try
To be found,
Hoping that I will meet happiness on common ground

Who am I, and why do I feel this way?
Why do I harbor feelings that I want to go away?

I'm so scared shaking in this corner of loneliness
Running from evil
God knows I don't want this.

Feel my tears and me empathetically
And if you are feeling the same
Then I render you my sympathy.

My secrets tunnel through the passages of my eyes
Hidden inside, formulating lies
That is truths
Truths, in which I despise

I hurt because I know my thoughts and desires are not right
But I hide out from the world in the mass
Asking god to fight this fight

I so eagerly want to be free to roam
And call my house a home.
I'm a child of god who needs to excel
And spread my wings and fly from this confinement
Like a beautiful angel

Say Something

By: Marcus Q Jackson

Say something that may spark my interest.
And change my view of how I perceive you
Say something even something senseless
You need not feel defenseless
But you must say something if you really want this

I can tell by your stare
Beneath the florescent glare
You're hoping that we can share
Romantic evenings alone ocean side
Rubbing your fingers through my silky long hair
Listening to the sounds of the tide

You must first say something
Ask me my name
Ask me where I'm from
Don't stand there looking dumb

Say something

What?
Are you afraid that I will reject
Or disrespect you the unconfident subject
Trying to protect his self-respect

Maybe it's that you're checking me out
Trying to feel me out
Creating assumptions as to what I'm really about
I seriously doubt
You will ever find out
What I'm really about

Staring out from the corner
As if you're some sort of bashful loner
My my my what ever happen to a mans honor
Come on offer me a drink
We can start there
Don't be cheap
Offer a sister more than a beer

I mean say something

What's wrong?
Is it my beautiful appearance? That has you skeptical and scared
Must be, can't be anything I've said
Confused so I turned my head

Here's this average but confident brother who wasn't afraid to speak
Hello my names Maleek
I'm honored that we could meet

Taking me by the hand
Walking me to his table gentleman like, pulling out my seat

Next to the loner in the corner
Who was afraid to speak

I Closed My Eyes

By: Marcus Q. Jackson

As I closed my eyes and rested upon my knees
Praying to God
Oh God this just can't be
Please Lord tell me that my mind is playing tricks on me
My love will never mess around on me
Fiction, for reality is a liar
She will never jeopardize her everlasting desire
And I closed my eyes, I closed my eyes
I closed my eyes but to my surprise
Fiction was fact
And I couldn't hold back my cries.
She's playing me, my love is playing me
Her truths were all lies
And I closed my eyes

Oh so he's a friend ya'll just cool
And you met at work,
So this e-mail I'm reading doesn't mean anything
When he said that he hurt
Cause you can't control having sex with me
And the fact that you haven't left me yet
So that he can have you all to himself
I closed my eyes
Because that line took away my breath

Baby what have you done how come this guy knows about me
How does he know please someone tell me?
He even knew when I moved in with my boy for that week

I closed my eyes
I closed my eyes
I closed my eyes

Honey, you said it's nothing
The guy is just crazy
Don't pay any attention to this craziness
Don't let some insane guy ruin our happiness
I took a deep breath and I closed my eyes and said
I believe you boo
Because I love you

And I closed my eyes with doubt,
I closed my eyes with doubt,
I closed my fucking eyes with doubt
Bug the phone bug the phone find out
What's going on?
I must know!! No I got to know!!
In fact I have the motherfucking right to know
What's really going on?

So I closed my eyes
I closed my eyes
I closed my eyes
Don't worry the coast is clear

Come over my man's beeping in on the phone
My son's asleep, his dad's at work
And I'm left here "Horny" all alone.

Hurry up don't worry about parking at the store
Down the street out of sight
You can park outside
My man will be at work all night.

Tears fell hard down my face
I plugged my ears to the disgrace
I closed my eye's to the disgrace
I closed my eyes to the disgrace
I closed my eyes to the disgrace.

No I yelled as I came through the window
You fucking ho
Ripping off her naked body the robe I bought
Noticing the a jarred front door
Where the fuck is he
Oh yeah homey come on out you bad
My heart was pounding
I was to hurt to feel sad
I closed my eyes got damn I'm mad
I closed my eyes damn it I'm mad

Lord stop me please take my hand from around her neck
Please don't let me kill her for the disrespect
To our home our son and to me

A pain I will never forget
Die bitch die
You know what
You're not even worth it.

I closed my eyes but they opened
I closed my eyes but they opened
I closed my eyes but they opened
To the sound of my love frantically choking
Leaving me heart broken
Hoping that this nightmare wasn't so
But reality set in when I saw her lovers' cell phone on my sofa
And the wind blowing leaves through my a jarred front door
"You ho"

I threw my love down on the desecrated furniture
You're lucky you lying cheating bitch
I should shake a deal with the reaper
Cause there's not a doubt that he wouldn't want you

I can't move
Why can't I move from this spot?
My tears excessively dropped
Watching the woman I love call the cops
Saying that I was trying to kill her
Slowly fading away my eyes were a blur
All I heard was yes sir yes sir

He's beating on me
I'm afraid he's walking around frantically
I grabbed the phone and threw it against the wall
And said when the cops come looking for me
Turn yourself in for murder in the first degree.
Because the dead can't kill I said walking towards the living room
door
Show them how you ripped out my heart and through it on the
living room floor
Tears disburse to my sadden demise
Looking back at my love
And
I closed my eyes.

Love

By: Marcus Q. Jackson

It's hard to walk burdened down by the pressures
Of love
An emotional roller coaster attacking the mind
And the chemistry there of

Love, love's no one it will catch you sleeping
If two hearts are not one love will leave someone weeping
It's precious when you give it but it hurts like hell when it
Boomerangs back because there was no one there to receive it,

Leaving you in pain grieving and confused
Leaving a feeling of hopelessness, giving up with the fear that
You will always loose.

It's hard to move in the quick sands of pain
Hoping that love will soon come and set you free
Instead love is the quick sand that's covering me.

Slowly sinking contemplating thinking
No answer from the divine
I call to the bottle
Excessively drinking

Where is this love that begged of me to be true?
Would this be the same love that has me feeling alone and blue?

How could you change love and disregard my place
Taking what I feel
And Regurgitate back in my face

I feel violated mislead and cheated
When you told me that my services were no longer needed

So it was just a ride and the journey is taking you elsewhere
Your look is of ice rendering this cold feel
A feel as if you never did care.

About the times we've shared and the memories lost
About the kids we bared and the possessions that cost
About the pain one felt being neglected
Or the hardening of your heart as I was
Blatantly disrespected

They say it is better to have loved and lost than not too have
Loved at all
I don't know about all that
But I know that love was my downfall

You gave no pre-warning, no sign of the end
I say again
Love you love no one and no longer could you be my friend.

A Time That Was

By: Marcus Q. Jackson

Hammocks swayed between the shade trees
A gentle breeze
Oceans sparkled from the sunlight above
A time that was
A time of love

High misty Mountain tops
Calm Rain forest dripping silent raindrops
As we laid
A time that was
A time engraved
Time that has passed away

Sweet coconut trees
Skinny-dipping in Waikiki
Her beautiful smooth caramel skin covered me
I held her tight
Under the Hawaiian moonlight
That lit up the night
A time that was
A time when things were just right

Biking through the exotic trails peacefully
She said no one could be

As happy as we
Sipping water resting under the palm tree

A time that was
A time taken for granted
I put a letter in a bottle and tossed it out to sea
Hoping that my love will soon come and find me

Plaza Hotel
New England clam chowder
A time that was
Now a time without her

Sunday drives around the island exploring
Quality Time
Passionate moments never boring
Waikele, 157 Curtis Court
A time that was a time of love
A time I shall never ignore.

That Old Familiar Song

By: Marcus Q. Jackson

Driftwood floats
On a wave, in a reverse current
Subtracted from reality to the subtle sound of song
Pleasing to the ears stimulating the brain
You remember the rain

Soft rain falling outside the window
Cuddled close
Fireplace, champagne, cashmere rug across the floor

Darkening skies blinded the earth
Gave way to the birth
Of song

As lightning struck the sky
The sound of thunder rolled by
A lady began to cry

In a sorrowful voice expounding sound
Murmured the words I'm going down
The effervescent of Asti rose to the top
Tingling sounds of crystal
Solid rain drops.

The sadness in her voice filled the room
She could not stop

Her passion for one amplified
The hearts of all around
She was crying because her man was not around
She yelled out
In a mournful sound, I'm going down.

Satin sheets passionate heat
Clinched hands furrowed feet
To the sounds of sadness
Of one's heart
Filled with loneliness so far apart

I hear the same sound
I smell the same rain
I see the same lightning
I can taste the same Champagne
I feel the voice of the stranger's pain
Every time I hear her sing

I'm going down because you're not around
A memorable sound
Driftwood floats upstream by the sea
Temporarily suspended from love life and reality

I Love You

By: Marcus Q. Jackson

I can't help myself
When I think of you my heart melts
Reminiscing on the feelings I once felt
And continue to feel
These feelings are surreal
I wish you near to dry my tears
How more defined shall I be
To make myself clear

I love you

Let it be known but not as a sadden occasion
But a day of celebration
To know that I could continue loving you
After this magnitude of devastation

I love you

Not mere words spoken in vane
But a feeling that nearly drove me insane
My tears fell like the rain
Enduring the pain
Through God
I found the strength to maintain
Yet things aren't the same

I love you

Forever you will be apart of me
The last Ruby red apple
Hanging from the Apple tree
The last drop of honey
From the Honey Bee
Can't you see what your love has done too me

I love you

Dream caster can't create a dream of how I feel
Je ne sais quoi, difficult to describe or express
These feelings I obtained are real
As the morning Sun
The glow of Rainbows the calm after the storm
When I met you a new me was born
You are the one.

I love you

Shot by the gun I decided to run
Tracked by past feelings that decided to come
What is this love and what has it done
Self love and love for others
Spilled over, mommy daughter siblings and son
All require some
Of my heart, but you hold the lump sum

I love you

Don't you get it, can't you see?
There's no branch without the tree
There's no bumble without the Bee
There's no Red without the Sea
So why should there be a you without the me.
It's like a disease baby please

I love you

Separated and devastated
Always willing to share this heart of love
Our God created
I stand as a man when shunned as the fool
Taking pride in saying baby
I love you cause I do.
I love you
There's no woman to take your place
There are no papers to erase
These feelings are forever
Like God and Grace
Look at me I love you
It's written all over my face
There's no limit to the things I would do
To hear you say again baby I love you.
I love you…I love you

Signs

By: Marcus Q. Jackson

How can I move on when every sign's the same?
More signs but this time it detours the brain
In search for the highway of love
Away from which I came

Hours of driving
Only to return to a place that looks the same
Yielding not a name
Frustration
Who shall I blame?
For this place that I've came

I've followed the signs
Patient with time
Now I'm running low on gas
Driving blind
In search for a new destination
And leave the old far behind
The lost map of life
I seek to find
To give me direction
To ease my mind

Flower gardens
Spring streams of sparkling dreams

Wishing wells
Fragrant smells
Honey dripping sunrays
Harmonic rings of Christian bells
Angels dancing on air
Autumn breeze
Through whispering trees
Melodic Lullabies
Casting spells of sleep
Aquatic fish dancing through the sea
Mirrors of freedom
Revealing images of me
At the oceans bank
Sipping tea
Under a cherry oak tree
Far as my eyes could see
I envision this place
This place I long to be
I need new signs
Post them upon the street
Signs that will help me find my way free

To the land of milk and honey
Where my worth is not compared to money
Everlasting love never lonely
Where everyone smiles and greets me
Like they have always known me.

Slowly I close the windows of pain
Awakening to the sound and the feel of refreshing rain
Basting my face
I opened my mouth to the taste
Of moisture dripping down my face
Once erased

Clouds drifted casually away in the eastern wind
My wings blossomed I was able to fly again
I soared through the sky to no end
Closer approaching my sunshine
Nervous yet anxious knowing not where to begin
A reunion with destiny reunited again

The warmth of the sun pierced my soul
The sparkle from her smile
Gave off a hypnotic glow
I have my sun back and never again will I let her go
She whispered I miss you
As she held me ever so close

I closed my eyes to the glow of sunlight and kiss her lips
Our love was the demise of the eclipse

Others

By: Marcus Q Jackson

Must one flaw be the demise of my life?
Must one choice be the decision of eternity?
Must one love be all that concerns me?
Must all fantasies become reality?
Must my eyes be the only one's used to see?
Must I judge myself to get to know me?
Must I be a fish to travel through the sea?

Must I bare alone all un-welcome troubles?
Is the truth of evolution
Sharing with others
And learn from others
And discover with others
Embrace like sisters and brothers
Reproduce as lovers
Melt together the colors
Brighten the duller
Truly amazing what we might discover
A protocol son a protocol brother
A mighty God hovers
Waiting to heel all un-desired troubles

Could we all be one unit of energy?
Descent to be
Love for eternity

Passionate in the depths of infinity
You hold the light
Look within the
And you will see
That your life holds all possibilities

Psalms 23

By: Marcus Q. Jackson

Some say life is simple
And love is just a silly thing
Happiness is the lyrics
In the songs we sing
And pleasure is a gift that money brings.
For those I say love doesn't mean a damn thing.

Hearts beat
But do you take the time out to listen
At the sounds that control your destiny
Listen, listen with compassion
Feel the passion unselfishly
Listen to me.

For I'm your heart that beats the rhythmic sound and more
Living within your beautiful body, feeding your unselfish mind
Seeing your reality through those shadowy eyes
I adore!! The shine

I need more, of you piece by piece
The rhythm of your heart
Beat by beat.

Surrender to my love and I shall teach you feel
Making all your dreams appear
And all your fears disappear.

For I'm your comforter,
I alone
A support beam that will give you the strength to stand strong
I will forever promise to be that comfort zone.

If ever you decide to place your hand within mine
Know that you could leave it there for the rest of time.
For I will never leave or forsake thee
I will continue to always give you the best of me.
A child of God, Psalms 23

I want love

By: Marcus Q. Jackson

I need to know about love
It's such a strange game
I really want to know about love
Knowing love is too know my own name
I want too be in love I want someone too love me the same
I want love
I want someone too hold my name

Why must I be alone?
In this world of grief
Why must I continue to believe?
That theirs that someone waiting for me
Is it so
Please let me no

I want love
I need love
I challenge love
I desire love
Love let me love you
And I will love you the same
Love please take my name

Lost, I'm lost out here on my on
Luther Vandross sings the song

Since I lost my baby
Since I lost my baby
I never was the same
Love
I ask you to remember my name

Unfurl

By: Marcus Q. Jackson

My heart melts like heated candle wax
I'm tired but I can't relax.
There's a race to run
Staring down the barrel of the gun.
Under fire at every given second alone in this world
Always out numbered always out gunned
My life unfurls.

To every needed hand
I try so hard to understand
The physical that we call man
The same man who will shoot me where I stand.

Why must I love you
Why do I even care
I hate this love, it takes me no where.

My eyes bleed from the deceit
I want to retreat
This life of disbelief
Please no more grief.

Be straight with me
Tell me that you're using me
My prayers God are you refusing me.

When I cry how come there's no one sent for me
To walk for me
Like the foot print poem adjacent the magazine

As I mourn
An emotional cry
For the human race
When faced with common disgrace
From this place
I try maintaining this rapid pace
To keep up before being erased
Amazing grace
How sweet it sound
Plant my feet on common ground
Tell me that I'm not alone and that you are always around.

Dismal thoughts as I sit and wait
Hoping if not you
Someone positive will soon come my way.

Lord I'm tired of being the answer to everyone
Removing the tension from their gun
As if I was the chosen one
Lord I call
Un-muzzled mouth I fall
Into the immure
Confined within walls

That spoke to me within a war fare to sin
Hebrew chapter two verses nine and ten.
The Explanation of life's long suffering.

ISBN 141203071-4

9 781412 030717

Cap
Crossbones
and the
Lost Treasure

Narinder Dhami

Illustrated by
Lucy Fleming

OXFORD
UNIVERSITY PRESS

OXFORD
UNIVERSITY PRESS

Great Clarendon Street, Oxford, OX2 6DP,
United Kingdom

Oxford University Press is a department of the University of Oxford.
It furthers the University's objective of excellence in research, scholarship,
and education by publishing worldwide. Oxford is a registered trade mark of
Oxford University Press in the UK and in certain other countries

British Library Cataloguing in Publication Data
Data available

978-0-19-837727-6

7 9 10 8 6

Paper used in the production of this book is a natural, recyclable product
made from wood grown in sustainable forests. The manufacturing process
conforms to the environmental regulations of the country of origin.

Printed in China by Leo Paper Products Ltd.

Acknowledgements
Inside cover notes written by Becca Heddle
Author photograph by RMH Media

Contents

Chapter 1
Vanished!

"My treasure is missing!" Captain Crossbones roared angrily. "Where, oh where, can it be?"

Captain Crossbones' real name was Emily, but she didn't like it when people called her that.

Captain Crossbones began to search her bedroom. It was one big mess. There were clothes and toys everywhere. Captain Crossbones looked in all the places she could think of, but her treasure had vanished. Vanished, just like that, into thin air!

"Someone's stolen my treasure," Captain Crossbones muttered, grabbing her cutlass. "Just wait till I find out who it is. I'll tie them to the ship's mast. I'll make them walk the plank. I'll feed them to the fishes!"

Captain Crossbones ran downstairs. Mum heard her and came out of the kitchen.

"Have you cleaned up your bedroom yet, Emily?" Mum asked.

"Shiver me timbers, Cook!" Captain Crossbones replied. "No, I haven't. My treasure's been stolen!"

"There'll be trouble if you don't tidy up that mess," Mum warned.

"Can we have fish and chips for dinner, Cook?" Captain Crossbones asked hopefully.

"Yes, but only if you tidy your bedroom!" Mum replied, and she went back into the kitchen.

"Oh no!" Captain Crossbones groaned. "I have to find my lost treasure quickly, so I have time to tidy my cabin before dinner. I need help. Where's my crew?"

Captain Crossbones whistled loudly. "Ahoy, Cut-throat Charlie!" she yelled.

Cut-throat Charlie trotted out of the living room, wagging his tail.

"We've got to find my lost treasure, Charlie," Captain Crossbones explained. "We'll need the help of Blood-thirsty Ben, the Terror of the Seven Seas!"

"Woof!" said Charlie.

Captain Crossbones knew Charlie
was saying, "We'll find your treasure,
Captain, even if we have to search for a
hundred years!"

"Come on, my faithful friend," said
Captain Crossbones. "We'll sail across
the sea to Blood-thirsty Ben's ship next
door and ask him to help."

Together, Captain Crossbones and Cut-throat Charlie hurried across the deck. But suddenly the bell rang.

"Who's this?" Captain Crossbones whispered. "Someone's trying to get on board our ship!"

"Woof!" said Charlie.

Captain Crossbones knew Charlie was saying, "We'll tie him up and feed him to the sharks!"

Chapter 2
Who Stole the Treasure?

"Ahoy there!" Captain Crossbones yelled.
"Tell me who you are or I won't let you
on board my ship. Are you friend or foe?"

"Friend!" shouted the person outside
the door.

"It's our friend, Charlie," Captain
Crossbones said. "It's Blood-thirsty Ben,
the Terror of the Seven Seas."

"Woof," said Cut-throat Charlie happily.

"Ahoy, Blood-thirsty Ben!" said
Captain Crossbones. "I need your help. A
scurvy thief has stolen all my treasure!"

Blood-thirsty Ben looked shocked.
"That's bad," he said.

"I have to find my missing treasure
and tidy my cabin before dinner,"
Captain Crossbones told him. "Or Cook
says I won't get any fish and chips."

"That's REALLY bad!" gasped
Blood-thirsty Ben.

"We'll search this ship from top to bottom," Captain Crossbones said. "We'll ask everyone on board if they've stolen my treasure."

"We'll make them talk by tickling their toes," said Ben with a blood-thirsty grin.

"It's a deadly and dangerous mission," the captain said. "Are you with me?"

"Aye-aye, Captain!" Ben shouted, and Charlie barked loudly.

Captain Crossbones and her crew began looking for the lost treasure in the kitchen.

"You're getting under my feet," Mum said. "Mind the flour!"

"A scurvy thief has stolen my treasure, Cook," Captain Crossbones growled. "Was it you?"

"No, Emily, it wasn't," Mum replied. "Now go and play somewhere else!"

Dad was vacuuming the hall floor.

"Ahoy, ship's mate!" said Captain Crossbones. "The deck looks nice and clean. Keep up the good work!"

"Mind your feet, Emily," said Dad.

"A scurvy thief has stolen all my treasure," Captain Crossbones growled. "Was it you?"

"No, Emily, it wasn't," Dad replied. "Now go and play somewhere else!"

"Let's ask the ship's parrot," said Captain Crossbones. "Ahoy, Poppy the parrot!"

Poppy looked rather cross. "What do you want, Emily?" she snapped. "Can't you see I'm on the phone?"

"You're always talking, Poppy!" Captain Crossbones growled. "Are you the scurvy thief who stole my treasure?"

"No, Emily, I'm not," Poppy replied. "Now go and play somewhere else!"

"The ship's cat might be the thief,"
Blood-thirsty Ben whispered.

"Grr!" Cut-throat Charlie growled at
the sleeping cat.

"No, it wasn't the ship's cat,"
Captain Crossbones replied. "I think I
know who stole my treasure!"

"Who?" Blood-thirsty Ben wanted
to know. "Was it the ship's cook? Was
it the ship's mate? Was it Poppy the
ship's parrot?"

Captain Crossbones shook her head.
"No, I don't think it was one of them,"
she said. "I think it was Oliver the
Terrible. I bet *he* took my treasure!"

"Oliver the Terrible?" Ben gasped.
"The most evil baddy in the whole world?"
"Yes," Captain Crossbones replied.

Chapter 3
Kidnapped!

Captain Crossbones, Blood-thirsty Ben and Cut-throat Charlie raced to the captain's cabin to find her spyglass.

"Your cabin's a bit of a mess, Captain," said Ben, looking around.

"Never mind that now!" Captain Crossbones snapped. "We *must* find Oliver the Terrible and get my treasure back!"

Captain Crossbones put the spyglass
to her eye and stared out across the sea.
She could see Oliver the Terrible's fort
not far away.

"I wonder if Oliver the Terrible is
hiding there?" Captain Crossbones said.

"Maybe that's where he's taken your
treasure!" replied Blood-thirsty Ben.

"Woof!" barked Cut-throat Charlie.

"We need a plan, Blood-thirsty Ben," said Captain Crossbones. "How am I going to get my treasure back from Oliver the Terrible?"

"WOOF!" Charlie barked at the top of his voice. "WOOF! WOOF! WOOF!"

Captain Crossbones and Blood-thirsty Ben turned around and saw that a note had been pushed under the cabin door.

"Good work, Cut-throat Charlie!" the captain whispered. "I think this might be one of Oliver the Terrible's tricks. Stand back while I take a look."

Captain Crossbones picked up the note and read it.

I HAVE KIDNAPPED ONE OF YOUR CREW.
ONE-EYED JACK IS A PRISONER IN MY FORT.
BRING ME TEN PIECES OF SILVER RIGHT AWAY, OR YOU'LL NEVER SEE ONE-EYED JACK AGAIN.
HA! HA! HA!
Signed, OLIVER THE TERRIBLE

"Oliver the Terrible has kidnapped One-Eyed Jack!" Captain Crossbones gasped. "And Oliver knows I can't pay ten pieces of silver because he stole my treasure! Didn't I tell you he was full of tricks?"

"Poor One-Eyed Jack," said Ben sadly. "What are we going to do now, Captain Crossbones?"

Chapter 4
The Plan

"I'll tell you what we're going to do," Captain Crossbones said. "We're going to storm Oliver the Terrible's fort. We're going to free One-Eyed Jack and get my treasure back!"

"Woof!" Cut-throat Charlie barked excitedly.

"Let's go right away!" Blood-thirsty Ben shouted.

"Not so fast," said Captain Crossbones. "First we must arm ourselves."

"Are you ready, Blood-thirsty Ben?"
Captain Crossbones cried.

"Ready, Captain," Ben replied.

"Ready, Cut-throat Charlie?" asked
Captain Crossbones.

"Woof," said Charlie.

"Just remember that Oliver the
Terrible is *very* bad and *very* clever,"
Captain Crossbones said. "He'll try all
kinds of tricks, and we must be ready
for him!"

"Is it all clear?" whispered
Captain Crossbones.

"All clear, Captain," Blood-thirsty
Ben replied.

"Let's go," Captain Crossbones told
them. "But stay close to me and look
out for Oliver the Terrible. He may be
spying on us. He may even try to attack
us first!"

Captain Crossbones, Blood-thirsty Ben and Cut-throat Charlie crept across the deck. All the time, they kept a sharp lookout for Oliver the Terrible.

Then suddenly a loud voice shouted, "WAIT!"

"You made us jump, Cook!"
Captain Crossbones gasped. "We're
on the lookout for Oliver the Terrible.
Have you seen him?"

"No, I haven't seen your brother,
Emily," Mum replied. "He could be
outside in the tree house. It's you I want
to talk to. Have you cleaned up your
bedroom yet?"

"I can't do it right now, Cook," Captain Crossbones groaned. "I'm on the trail of my stolen treasure."

"I'll check your room at six o'clock, Emily," said Cook. "And if it's still a mess, then no fish and chips for you!"

Captain Crossbones looked at the ship's clock. It was half past five.

"Shiver me timbers!" Captain Crossbones gasped. "There's no time to waste."

Chapter 5
The Attack

Captain Crossbones, Blood-thirsty Ben
and Cut-throat Charlie set off towards
the fort.

"Ssh, don't make a sound," the
captain said. "We're going to attack
Oliver the Terrible in his fort and take
him by surprise."

Soon the captain, Ben and Charlie were standing under the tree house. They could hear loud, crunchy noises coming from inside.

"What's Oliver the Terrible doing up there?" Blood-thirsty Ben whispered.

"I hope One-Eyed Jack is all right," Captain Crossbones said with a frown. "Let's go and rescue him!"

The captain, Ben and Charlie burst into the fort.

"We've come to rescue our crewmate, One-Eyed Jack!" Captain Crossbones roared. "And to get my treasure back!"

Oliver the Terrible jumped to his feet and dropped the big bag of crisps he was eating.

"Never!" he shouted. "I'll never give up One-Eyed Jack. He's my prisoner!"

Captain Crossbones and Blood-thirsty Ben tried to grab Oliver the Terrible, but he was big and strong. He got away from them, and the three pirates began to fight.

"Grr!" Cut-throat Charlie growled at the cat. The cat arched her back and hissed. Then she chased Charlie around the fort.

"Let One-Eyed Jack go, or you'll be sorry, Oliver the Terrible!" Captain Crossbones snarled. "And I want my treasure back too, you scurvy thief!"

"I didn't steal your treasure," Oliver replied. "But I *do* have One-Eyed Jack, and he's staying here until I get my ten pieces of silver!"

"You go and look for my treasure,
Ben," Captain Crossbones shouted.
"Leave Oliver the Terrible to me."

"Aye-aye, Captain," Blood-thirsty
Ben replied, and he ran off to search the
fort for the captain's treasure.

Suddenly, Captain Crossbones spotted One-Eyed Jack. She ducked past Oliver the Terrible and ran to the other side of the fort. Then she grabbed One-Eyed Jack and gave him a big hug.

"Jack, I'm so glad you're safe," Captain Crossbones gasped. "Blood-thirsty Ben, did you find my treasure?"

"It's not here, Captain," Ben said. "I've looked everywhere."

"Stay away from my fort from now on!" Oliver the Terrible shouted. "Or next time I'll tie you up and tickle you till you can't speak! I'll spin you around until you're so dizzy, you can't see straight!"

"Well, we got One-Eyed Jack
back," said Captain Crossbones. "That's
good. But we didn't find my treasure.
That's bad."

"And we still don't know who stole
the treasure," Blood-thirsty Ben replied.

Captain Crossbones, Blood-thirsty Ben, Cut-throat Charlie and One-Eyed Jack hurried back to the pirate ship.

When they reached the deck, Captain Crossbones looked at the ship's clock.

It was ten minutes to six.

"I've got to tidy my cabin now, before Cook comes to check at six o'clock." Captain Crossbones groaned. "Or there'll be no fish and chips for dinner!"

Chapter 6
Fish and Chips for Dinner

Captain Crossbones, Ben and Charlie rushed to the captain's cabin.

"Do you think we've got time to clean things up in ten minutes?" Captain Crossbones asked hopefully.

"No way," Blood-thirsty Ben said, sitting down on the bed. "It's much too messy!"

"Woof!" Cut-throat Charlie barked sadly.

"Ouch!" Ben gasped, jumping up
again. "I just sat down on something
hard and sharp."

"Did you hurt yourself, Ben?" asked
Captain Crossbones. "What did you
sit on?"

"I don't know," Ben said with a frown.
"It's hidden under this pile of clothes."

Captain Crossbones and Ben pulled all the clothes off the bed to find out what he'd sat on.

"It's my missing treasure!" Captain Crossbones yelled happily. "Now I remember! I was going to count my gold and silver when I was in bed this morning. But I got up to take Charlie for a walk, and I forgot."

"So we got One-Eyed Jack back *and* we found my treasure," said Captain Crossbones. "But now we only have *five* minutes left to tidy my cabin before six o'clock."

"No fish and chips for you, Captain," Ben said sadly.

"Maybe it's not too late," Captain Crossbones said with a big smile. "I have an idea!"

"Emily, I'm coming to check your room," Mum called as she went upstairs. "If everything's clean and tidy, then I'll send your dad to buy fish and chips for dinner. But if your room's still a mess, then it's cheese on toast for you!"

"My cabin's really tidy, isn't it, Cook?" said Captain Crossbones proudly. "So can we have fish and chips, please?"

"Yes, we can," said Mum. "Would you like to stay for dinner, Ben?"

"Yes, please," Blood-thirsty Ben said eagerly.

"Woof," said Cut-throat Charlie.

"You can have fish and chips, too, Charlie!" said Mum.

"We found my lost treasure, we won our fight with Oliver the Terrible *and* we're having fish and chips for dinner," Captain Crossbones said happily. She hugged One-Eyed Jack. "It's great fun being a pirate!"

About the author

When I was a little girl like Emily, I loved stories about pirates. I remember once when we had to do a project at school. All of my friends were choosing fluffy kittens or cute puppies or ponies or ballet dancers for their projects. But I chose pirates!

I grew up dreaming of becoming a writer and then one day, after a lot of hard work, my dream came true. I've written hundreds of books about girls and boys and fairies and wizards and cats and dogs. But one day I realized that I'd *never* written a book about a pirate.

So here it is!